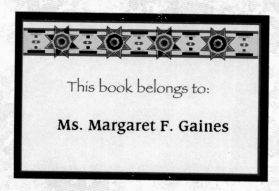

This book belongs to:

Ms. Margaret F. Gaines

By Roxie Kelley

With Illustrations by Shelly Reeves Smith

**Andrews McMeel
Publishing**

Kansas City

00 01 02 03 04 TWP 10 9 8 7 6 5 4 3 2 1
ISBN: 0-7407-1068-0

PRESENTED TO

FROM

To Mr. and Mrs. Chiles,
for showing me how to
find my home within.

—RGK

To Don, with love.
Home is wherever you are.

—SRS

a quieter or more untroubled retreat... than his own soul. "Nowhere can man find...

MARCUS · AURELIUS

It has been said...

"Home is where
the heart is."

HOME

is where the the

HEART

is

Shelly Reeves Smith

But home is really so much more.

Home Tweet Home

GARDEN

Home is where
the heart finds
comfort...

And peace...
and pleasure.

Along life's way
we discover...

Houses
hold
things.

But home is something altogether different.

The best things in life aren't things.

Home is where we learn how to laugh.

It is where we
welcome
souls.

It is the place
where broken hearts
are mended.

And dreams
are nurtured.

It grows outside
of its own
boundaries.

A real home
draws in
its own

With all the ease
of a
warm
embrace.

It pulls in
the
very
breath of life.

And releases that breath
just as peacefully.

To our brightest
and
best hopes,

And where we find the courage to pursue them.

The best home
creates its own
climate
within.

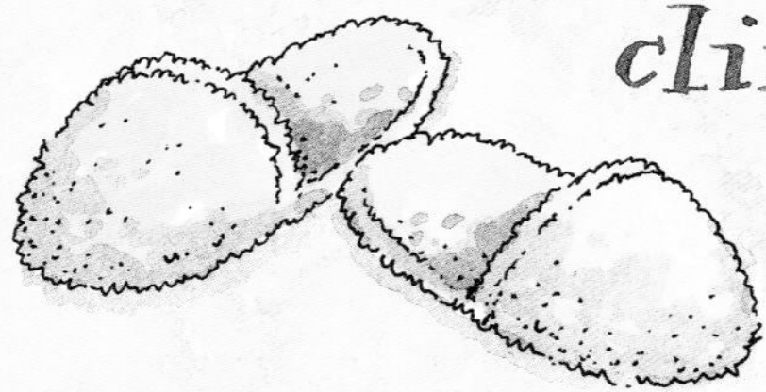

Independent of
the
forces of
nature...

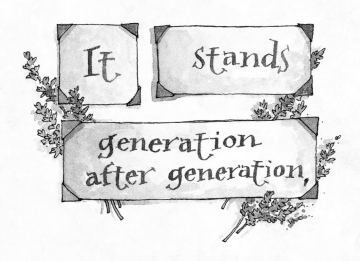

It stands generation after generation,

On the firmest of foundations...

A foundation
of character
and energy,

And of love
and
trust.

Most of all,

Home is
within us,
now
and always.